Toffee Marmalade

TWO PET STORIES

Kes Gray
Linda Jennings

Illustrated by
Dee Shulman

OXFORD
UNIVERSITY PRESS

OXFORD
UNIVERSITY PRESS

Great Clarendon Street, Oxford, OX2 6DP,
United Kingdom

Oxford University Press is a department of the University of Oxford.
It furthers the University's objective of excellence in research, scholarship,
and education by publishing worldwide. Oxford is a registered trade mark of
Oxford University Press in the UK and in certain other countries

British Library Cataloguing in Publication Data
Data available

978-0-19-837738-2

1 3 5 7 9 10 8 6 4 2

Paper used in the production of this book is a natural, recyclable product
made from wood grown in sustainable forests. The manufacturing process
conforms to the environmental regulations of the country of origin.

Printed in China by Leo Paper Products Ltd.

Acknowledgements
Cover and inside illustrations by Dee Shulman
Inside cover notes written by Becca Heddle

Contents

Crunch Time for Toffee

Kes Gray

Chapter 1

Toffee had been a bad dog.

She had eaten a whole bag of
dog treats and it wasn't even her dinner
time.

"Bad dog, Toffee!" said Dad.

"Bad, greedy dog, Toffee!" said Mum.

"Woof!" said Baby Andrew.

Mum, Dad and Toffee looked at Baby Andrew. He was sitting on the kitchen floor with a tennis ball in his mouth.

He dropped the ball on the floor and then barked again.

"Woof, woof, woof, woof!" he yapped, as the ball rolled across the kitchen floor towards the empty bag of dog treats.

Mum looked at Dad. Dad looked at Toffee, and then everyone looked at Baby Andrew again.

Now he was lying on his back with his legs in the air, waiting for his tum to be tickled.

"Goodness gracious," said Mum. "It isn't Toffee that's eaten a whole bag of dog treats. It's Baby Andrew!"

Dad picked up the empty Doggybix bag.

"Read what it says on the bag," said Mum. She was starting to panic.

Dad put his reading glasses on and peered at the writing on the bag.

Baby Andrew's mum clasped her hand to her mouth.

Oh my word! They've brought out the dog in Baby Andrew!

"Woof, woof!"

Baby Andrew sprang on to all fours.

He scratched himself with his back leg and then scampered up the hallway.

"What else does it say on the bag?" said Mum.

Baby Andrew's dad lifted the small writing closer to his glasses.

"It says, '*For extra bounce and vitality,*'" he said.

"Extra bounce and vitality? What does that mean?" said Baby Andrew's mum.

"I think *that's* what it means," said
Dad, pointing down the hallway.

Baby Andrew was running around and
around in circles, chasing his nappy.

He stopped for a moment and barked
with excited eyes at Mum, Dad and
Toffee.

Then he bounded up the stairs.

Mum, Dad and Toffee bounded after him.

"What are we going to do?" said
Mum, as Baby Andrew started scratching
at the bedroom door.

"How are we going to stop him?" said
Dad.

"There's no stopping him now,"
thought Toffee.

Those Doggybix are the best!

Toffee was right. There was no
stopping Baby Andrew.

All Mum, Dad and Toffee could do was watch, as Baby Andrew scampered from one room to another.

In the living room, they found Baby Andrew chewing the sofa.

GRRR!

In the nursery, he gnawed the ears off his squeaky toys.

In the garden, he even chased the neighbour's cat up a tree.

"Sit!" said Baby Andrew's dad in desperation, as Baby Andrew started digging up the lawn.

"Heel!" said Baby Andrew's mum, as Baby Andrew ran into the house and did a puddle on the carpet.

"What are we going to do?" said Baby Andrew's mum. "He should be doing baby things, not doggy things."

Toffee wasn't so sure. She quite liked the idea of having another dog around the house.

"I know what we must do," said Baby Andrew's dad. "We must take him to the doctor."

"Yes, we must take him to the doctor," said Baby Andrew's mum.

And take him to the doctor they did.

The doctor looked long and hard at Baby Andrew's tongue.

"Does he always dangle it out of his mouth like that?"

"Only since he's been a dog," sighed Baby Andrew's mum.

The doctor continued his examination.

When he asked Baby Andrew to say, "Aah," Baby Andrew said, "Woof."

When he tried to look down Baby Andrew's throat, Baby Andrew started licking his face.

And when he tried to listen to his chest, Baby Andrew rolled over on his back and started panting, loudly.

"You need to take him to a vet," said the doctor, folding up his stethoscope.

"Yes, we need to take him to a vet," said Baby Andrew's mum to Baby Andrew's dad.

So take him to the vet they did.

The vet lifted Baby Andrew up on to her table and gave him a careful examination.

WOOF!

"Is there a cure?" asked Baby Andrew's mum. "Can anything be done to make him better?"

The vet looked long and hard at Baby Andrew.

"I'm afraid there is only one thing I can suggest," said the vet.

If Baby Andrew isn't well again by the morning, Toffee will have to go.

GRRR!

Mum and Dad gasped. Toffee would have to go?

We can't get rid of Toffee. She's our dog. She's our little dog! She's our lovely, good, Toffee dog!

But the vet was deadly serious.

"It's because Toffee is a dog that she will have to go. Baby Andrew is copying every doggy move she makes. As long as there is a dog in the house, Baby Andrew will never stop doing doggy things."

Mum and Dad looked sadly at Baby Andrew and then miserably at Toffee.

Toffee didn't know where to look.

The vet lifted Baby Andrew down from the table, and Toffee and her family returned home.

Dad sat glumly in the armchair with Baby Andrew curled up at his feet.

"I'm sure he'll be his normal baby self by the morning," said Mum, placing a bowl of water on the carpet.

"I'm sure Toffee won't have to go," said Dad.

"Yes, we're sure you won't have to go," said Mum, stroking Toffee's head.

"I'm not taking any chances," thought Toffee.

Chapter 2

That night, Mum and Dad tucked Baby Andrew up in his new dog basket.

They were exhausted. They went upstairs to bed and were soon snoring loudly.

Toffee went into action.

She went over to where Baby Andrew was sleeping and gave him a nudge.

Baby Andrew woke up and gave an
excited "Woof" when he saw Toffee.

Toffee wagged her tail at Baby
Andrew and then scampered into the
kitchen.

Baby Andrew scampered after her, just
as Toffee hoped he would.

Once inside the kitchen, Toffee pushed
the door closed with her nose. She sat
down in front of Baby Andrew.

Just as Toffee hoped he would, Baby
Andrew sat down in front of Toffee.

Toffee looked at Baby Andrew. Baby Andrew looked at Toffee.

Toffee woofed. Baby Andrew woofed.

Toffee sniffed. Baby Andrew sniffed.

Toffee scratched her left ear. Baby Andrew scratched his left ear.

Toffee stood up on two legs and walked over to the kitchen drawer.

Baby Andrew stood up and followed her.

Toffee took out a bib and placed it
over her head and then handed one to
Baby Andrew.

She took two breakfast bowls from
the shelf, a carton of milk from the
fridge and two breakfast spoons from
the drawer.

"Woof!" said Baby Andrew, excitedly.

"Gurgle," said Toffee. "Goo-goo, gurgle, ga-ga burble."

Baby Andrew listened carefully and then smiled. "Gurgle," he said. "Goo-goo, gurgle, ga-ga burble."

"That's more like it," thought Toffee, climbing into the high chair.

Baby Andrew climbed into the high chair with Toffee. He waited to see what she would do next.

Toffee picked up a breakfast spoon and poured milk and cereal into a bowl. Baby Andrew did the same.

Toffee put a spoonful of crunchy flakes into her mouth.

Baby Andrew did the same.

Toffee reached for some sugar, sprinkled it on her crunchy flakes and gurgled.

Baby Andrew did the same.

Toffee burped.

Baby Andrew burped.

Toffee threw a spoonful on to the floor, just for fun.

Baby Andrew did the same.

Spoonful by spoonful, Toffee emptied her breakfast bowl.

Spoonful by spoonful, Baby Andrew did the same.

Toffee climbed down from the high chair.

Baby Andrew did the same.

Toffee played with the fridge magnets.
Baby Andrew did the same.

"This is going to work!" thought
Toffee. "It's really going to work!"

The next morning, Baby Andrew's
mum and dad woke to the sound of loud
woof-woof-woofing.

Mum gripped the bed sheets and
looked anxiously at Dad.

"Is that Toffee – or is it Baby Andrew
barking at the postman?" said Mum.

Mum and Dad crept to the top of the stairs and peered down.

Toffee was sitting on the doormat, wagging her tail excitedly.

Mum and Dad walked down the stairs and patted Toffee on the head.

They then crept into the living room and closed the door behind them.

Toffee sat outside the door and waited.

Ten minutes later (seventy minutes in doggy years) the living room door sprang open. Baby Andrew's mum and dad came dancing out.

"Toffee, it's good news! It's fantastic news! Baby Andrew is Baby Andrew again and you don't have to go!" cried Dad.

"Yes! You can stay, Toffee!" smiled Mum. "You can stay! Baby Andrew isn't doing doggy things any more! He's doing baby things. He's doing amazing things! He's walking and gurgling and burbling again."

"And guess what, Toffee!" said Dad.

"He can spell 'Doggybix' with the magnets, and he can spell 'walkies' and 'lamp post.' He can even write a whole sentence: *'Top breeders recommend it.'*"

"It's incredible," said Mum, happily.

"It's a marvel!" said Dad.

"Goo-goo-goo, I mean, woof-woof-woof!" said Toffee.

A Cat Too Many

Linda Jennings

Chapter 1

"There's only one kitten not taken," said Mrs Tidy. "That one."

The tabby kitten was tiny, even for two weeks. A scrap of a thing, with a white face.

"Can I pick her up?" asked Nikky.

"Better not," said Mrs Tidy. "She's still too small."

Mrs Tidy had seven cats, as well as the mother cat and her four kittens. The room smelled of cats and fish, and Nikky's mother wrinkled her nose.

"Perhaps we'll leave her until she's six weeks old. Then we'll come to collect her — " she began, but Nikky tugged at her sleeve.

"No, Mum," she pleaded.

Nikky didn't care about Mrs Tidy's room smelling of cats and fish. She was crazy about cats.

"I wish we had a house like Mrs Tidy's," she said, as they walked home.

I'd like hundreds of cats.

"One's quite enough," said Mum. "You'll have to look after it, you know."

"Of course I will," said Nikky. "I know all about worming and grooming, and litter boxes and —"

"OK," said Mum, laughing. "I believe you."

They reached their front door. They
lived above Jim Mackenzie's corner shop.
There was a ginger cat living among the
wooden crates on the pavement.

Jim Mackenzie had made a bed for it
in a crate marked *Best Apples*. It wasn't
his cat, he explained, but it kept the mice
away.

Nikky stooped down to look inside the
crate and two large, green eyes stared out
at her.

When Nikky first saw him, the cat had spat at her. Now he knew her, and a purr rumbled in his throat.

Nikky knew better than to stroke him, though. Mum had warned her that stray cats had often been badly treated. They might lash out.

"Poor thing," said Nikky. "I wonder if he's got enough to eat?"

"I think so," said Mum, opening the door. Given half a chance, she knew that Nikky would bring him cans of cat food every day.

Next day, Nikky went with Mum to buy a collar for her new kitten with her pocket money. When they got back, Nikky looked into the crate as usual. The ginger cat stared out at her, green eyes squinting, and spat.

"That's funny, Mum," said Nikky. "He hasn't done that for ages."

"Got out of his crate the wrong side, I expect," said Mum.

"Cat's been like that all morning," said
Jim Mackenzie. "It won't let me near it."
Just then, Nikky saw bloodstained
paw marks on the pavement.

"Mum!" she shouted. "I think the cat's
been hurt."

Gently, Jim pulled the crate towards him. The cat whimpered with pain.

"Car accident, I reckon," said Jim. "But I'm too busy to take it to the vet. It's not really mine, anyway."

Nikky stared at the shopkeeper in horror.

But you can't just leave him!

Jim Mackenzie didn't seem to care.

"It'll be OK. These old strays are tough," he said.

"Come on, Nikky," said Mum. "Jim's right. We can't do anything."

"Nobody cares about a poor old cat without a home," thought Nikky.

As Mum pulled her unwillingly inside, she looked back. She thought she saw a ginger head poking out from the crate, but she couldn't really see through her tears.

Nikky worried about the cat all day.

Mum was worried too, and she told Dad about it. She explained how difficult it would be to catch the cat and take him to the vet.

"You're right," said Dad. "He'd probably struggle, and you'd do more harm than good. I expect Jim will call the cat rescue. It might be kindest for the cat to be put down if he is in a lot of pain."

"Put him down?" Nikky stared at Dad in horror. She ran into her bedroom, slamming the door.

Then she made up her mind. She would smuggle the cat upstairs to her bedroom. She would look after him, until he was better.

Nikky took her new cat basket from the cupboard. She knew Mum would be angry. But this was an emergency! Very quietly, she slipped down the stairs.

The cat was still there.

His bad leg looked all red and bloody, and flies were buzzing round it. Nikky felt a bit sick.

"Come on, Kitty," she said quietly, opening the basket.

"Did your Mum send you down?"
asked Jim Mackenzie, coming over to her.

"Er, no," said Nikky uncomfortably.
She couldn't tell him a lie.

But if no one's going to help the poor cat, I am!

"I'd like to know how," said Jim.
"Anyway, I've already phoned the cat
rescue. They're going to take him away."

Just as Mum and Dad said!

Nikky tipped the crate forward so that the cat would slide out into the cat basket. But before she could do anything, he scrambled out, dragging his wounded leg behind him.

Then he jumped over the wall and into one of the gardens. It must have hurt him terribly.

"Nikky!" Mum came down the stairs. She had seen Nikky talking to Jim. She grabbed her angrily by the arm.

"What do you think you're doing?"

"The cat — " began Nikky, and Mum suddenly shouted at her.

"The cat – that's all you think about, isn't it? Well, let me tell you, if there's any more of this nonsense, you won't even have a kitten!"

Afterwards, Mum was a bit sorry. She sat Nikky down with a drink and talked to her.

He's a tough old stray cat and he can fend for himself.

"You don't mean it about the kitten, do you?" asked Nikky. She felt like crying.

"Of course not – but calm down, will you? Try to think of something else but that old cat and the kitten."

That night, Nikky wasn't thinking of her kitten.

She was wondering what would happen if the ginger cat turned up again. How could she stop him from being put down?

Chapter 2

Outside, it had begun to rain. Nikky hoped the cat had found shelter. She hoped that his leg wasn't any worse.

Miaow!

What was that?

Nikky's heart began to thump. She opened the window, straining to see outside.

And there it was — a cat with a bad leg, crawling out from the shadows.

Nikky pulled on her dressing gown and dashed out of her bedroom.

Mum! Dad! The cat from downstairs! He's in our garden!

"Nikky, for goodness sake —" began Mum.

"Wait," said Dad. "She may be right. I thought I heard a cat crying. I'll go out and see."

Dad grabbed a torch and hurried downstairs. He opened the back door.

"Well, I never!" he said quietly to Nikky, who had followed behind him. "Just look at this!"

The ginger cat was crouched by the door. He drew back as Dad shone the torch, but he did not run away.

"*Now* what?" said Mum, looking over Dad's shoulder. "You'd better call the cat rescue. We can't look after it."

"Why not?" Nikky almost shouted. "We can't let them take him away – they might put him down – you said so."

"The cat rescue cares about animals," said Dad. "They would only do what was best for him."

The cat suddenly slid behind them, crawled upstairs, through the open door and into the kitchen. He crouched in the corner beside the fridge.

"I'll call them now – there must be an emergency number," said Dad.

Nikky grabbed hold of his arm. "You *can't* send him away, Dad. He's come to us. He thinks we'll look after him."

"Don't be silly, Nikky, he's only a cat – how can he possibly think anything?"

Nikky crouched down beside the cat and held out her hand. He snuffled at it with his damp, pink nose. Then he began to purr.

"Dad, look, he trusts me! Don't phone the cat rescue, please."

But Dad was already dialling.

"Hello?" he said.

Is that Dr Morgan's Emergency Service? I wonder if you could help me?

Nikky gave one big, happy sigh. Dad hadn't phoned the cat rescue. Dr Morgan was the vet!

The vet told Dad to keep the cat warm and dry and to give him fresh water and something to eat.

Mum sighed heavily as she opened a can of salmon.

"I hope you know what you're doing," she said.

We can't keep him. Nikky's having the kitten, remember? We haven't got room for two cats.

Nikky watched the cat, as he crawled painfully from the corner and began to nibble at the salmon. He ate slowly and neatly, not as if he were hungry at all. He left half of it.

"That's cats for you," said Dad. "Best red salmon, and it turns up its nose."

"It's the shock," said Nikky, who had read all about cats.

And he's probably not used to salmon.

"I bet not – but that's enough for tonight, Nikky. Off to bed!" said Dad.

Nikky lay for ages thinking about the ginger cat. How funny that he knew she lived upstairs! But what now?

She knew Mum wouldn't change her mind. She didn't like cats much, and they made her sneeze.

At last Nikky fell asleep to the sound of the rain beating against the windowpane.

Next morning, the cat let Dad pick him up and put him in the cat basket.

"He's been someone's pet at some time," said Dad. "You can see that."

"He's a strong cat," said Dr Morgan, when he examined him.

The vet cleaned the wound on the leg and gave him an injection.

"It's a nasty wound, but there are no bones broken," he said, cheerfully. "Bring him back in four days' time."

Mum looked at the signs on the vet's board. There were lots of people who needed cats and kittens.

KITTENS REQUIRED

ᴠᴠᴠ ᴍ ᴍ
ᴍᴍ ᴍᴍᴍ ᴨ
ᴀᴍ ᴠᴍ ᴠ

PLEASE PHONE
PET'S PARADISE

ᴍᴍᴍ ᴍ

Good home offered for kitten – any colour.

Phone
Mrs Fluff: *ᴜᴠᴢᴜ ᴜᴠᴠ*

Young cat or kitten wanted for children. Please phone Mr and Mrs Cosy:

ᴜ ᴨ ᴧ - .

**Kitten -
male or female
WANTED!**

Please phone
Ernest Plee:
ᴨᴍ ᴨ ᴨᴠ ᴨ

Nice family offers home to cat - black and white preferred.

ᴧᴍ ᴠᴍ ᴠ

"Good!" she said. "Once his leg's healed, we can put up a sign."

Day by day, the cat's leg grew better. He had a loud, deep purr, and he wound himself around Nikky's legs, and around her heart. She decided to call him Marmalade.

Sometimes, Marmalade would miaow softly at Nikky's bedroom door. And in the morning, Mum would find him curled up on Nikky's bed.

"I guess the next visit to Dr Morgan will be the last," said Mum. "I'll put up a sign on his board."

When no one had replied to the sign within a week, Mum sighed.

No one wants an older cat. Especially a big ugly cat like that.

Nikky picked up Marmalade and cuddled him. "He's not ugly! He's beautiful," she said. "Anyway, I don't want him to go."

"Nikky," warned Mum. "You know what we said. You can't have a kitten *and* Marmalade."

Nikky knew – and she had a big decision to make.

She went to see her kitten several times. The kitten was still very small and wobbled around the room after her big, black brother. She had huge eyes and a heart-shaped face. Nikky loved her – but the kitten needed her big brother, and Marmalade needed Nikky.

It was Mrs Tidy who helped Nikky
decide.

"The people who want the black kitten
would like the tabby one, too," she told
Nikky. "I said I didn't think you'd give
her up, but —"

Nikky picked up her kitten for the last
time and snuggled the kitten against her
neck.

The kitten licked her with a tiny,
pink tongue.

"It's all right," Nikky whispered. "They can have her — it will be best, really, seeing she's so small."

She followed Mum out, without looking back. On the way home, Mum bought a new blue collar. The one they'd bought for the kitten would be too small for Marmalade's big neck.

Marmalade was sitting on the doorstep outside the flat, waiting for them. And Nikky could swear there was a smile on his big, square face as he followed them upstairs for his dinner.

About the authors

Kes Gray writes:

What gave me the idea for *Crunch Time for Toffee?*

I am not sure, really, except we do have two dogs in our family and the week I wrote this story, our baby daughter Elsie was born.

Dogs and babies? Babies and dogs?

Linda Jennings writes:

Like Nikky, I am mad about cats and I have five of my own.

Unwanted cats can be so sad and this is why I wrote about Marmalade in *A Cat Too Many*.